RICHARD M JONES

THE
BURTON AGNES
DISASTER

THE FORGOTTEN WARTIME RAIL TRAGEDY
WHICH KILLED TWELVE INNOCENT MEN

RICHARD M JONES

THE
BURTON AGNES
DISASTER

THE FORGOTTEN WARTIME RAIL TRAGEDY
WHICH KILLED TWELVE INNOCENT MEN

MEREO
Cirencester

Mereo Books

1A The Wool Market Dyer Street Cirencester Gloucestershire GL7 2PR
An imprint of Memoirs Publishing www.mereobooks.com

The Burton Agnes Disaster: 978-1-86151-196-6

First published in Great Britain in 2014
by Mereo Books, an imprint of Memoirs Publishing

The address for Memoirs Publishing Group Limited can be found at
www.memoirspublishing.com

The Memoirs Publishing Group Ltd Reg. No. 7834348

The Memoirs Publishing Group supports both The Forest Stewardship Council® (FSC®) and
the PEFC® leading international forest-certification organisations. Our books carrying both the
FSC label and the PEFC® and are printed on FSC®-certified paper. FSC® is the only
forest-certification scheme supported by the leading environmental organisations including
Greenpeace. Our paper procurement policy can be found at
www.memoirspublishing.com/environment

Typeset in 11.5/17pt Book Antiqua
by Wiltshire Associates Publisher Services Ltd. Printed and bound in Great Britain by
Printondemand-Worldwide, Peterborough PE2 6XD

Contents

Chapter 1

Aftermath of war

The Second World War was an event that affected almost every human being alive. From those being called up to serve their duty to those being left at home to keep the country running, everybody had some reason to mourn a loss and had several major events occur that would alter their lives forever.

From the Battle of Britain to the sinking of the Bismarck, families all over were getting telegrams to say that their loved ones had been lost in action or taken prisoner in a far away and hostile land. From the outbreak of hostilities in 1939 until the war ended in 1945 Britain had been beaten black and blue, yet still came back up fighting, which led to the incredible push back of the Nazi war machine and the eventual defeat of Hitler by Allied forces.

The years after were spent counting the cost in lives, materials, buildings, ships, military equipment and normal everyday neighbourhoods. Every day of war was another day of loss, even if you were the winning side. When a ship sank it would take much-needed supplies, war materials, people and fuel. The effects of just one incident can be catastrophic - major missions put back several months, a lack of crucial materials to replace those which have already been lost and the skills of the people now no longer available. This required more effort to regain what had been lost, train new crews, replace vital transportation and even recall crucial paperwork to make sure vital information was not lost.

This was not just a daily struggle, but an hourly one. The shock of the toll of these losses devastated every county that was involved. Scandals erupted when the stories of Nazi war crimes hit the headlines as well as the stories of missions and accidents that had been kept secret for the sake of morale. In one case 173 people had been killed in a stampede in the heart of London when panic erupted at Bethnal Green subway after reports of a bombing raid. Something as big as this was completely blacked out until the time was right to tell the country. Even today people are still shocked by new wartime revelations.

During the war around 400,000 German soldiers, sailors and airmen came into the clutches of the British as prisoners of war. Shot down or captured on missions, they were sent away to hundreds of camps around the UK, or in some cases taken by ship over to Canada, to finish the remaining years of the war under the rule of prison guards.

This may sound like hell on earth, but in many cases the prisoners were glad that their war was over; they could make themselves busy and enjoy the English countryside while the major cities of both Britain and Germany burned on a nightly basis. Hitler's bombers wrought havoc on all the major areas of the UK. London and Coventry, Hull and Portsmouth - no built-up area was safe from the incendiaries and explosives that rained down from countless waves of aircraft. Time and time again these raids would devastate the cities, thousands would be killed, even more would be made homeless. It was only when the tide turned that the raids ended and the fight back was won.

For the prisoners of war, no longer were they in any danger fighting against sometimes impossible odds, although by 1945 a lot of them realised that there was nothing much left of the life they had left behind. Years of Allied bombing raids and eventual invasion by forces from Britain, Russia and the USA had split Germany in two. Towns and cities like Berlin and Dresden had been completely levelled to just piles of rubble. There was nothing to go home to, and many prisoners felt at a loss as to what to do once they were released.

By 1947, although two years had passed since the end of the war, many camps were still running with PoWs and using them in the countryside for various kinds of work in farms and villages. There was a delay in returning many prisoners long after the war was over, because of concern that they might live in the Russian sector of Germany and in turn become part of the communists, a part of history that was now being called the "Cold War."

Chapter 2

A tragedy in the making

One such camp running with these work programmes was Camp No 250 at Rudston on the East Yorkshire coast. Just a few miles away from the seaside town of Bridlington, Rudston is a tiny village surrounded by fields and farms, with a village pub and boasting the largest free-standing ancient stone anywhere in the UK, which is to be found in the local churchyard. The camp itself was divided among several areas of the village, including accommodation huts and even a hospital.

Dick Robinson was a local who remembers the camp very well. The army first started taking over the village in 1939 with the arrival of the Pioneer Corps, before the camp was built several years later. In a nearby wood were hidden a battery of 6-inch guns which propelled rounds towards Bridlington Bay several miles away. Week after week more and more wartime sights were seen in the small villages and towns nearby. Heavily-wooded areas provided good cover and shelter for training serials and to hide equipment from the eagle eyes of the German bombers.

The local town of Bridlington suffered air raids on the shops and houses. The railway lines and roads were targeted by those aircraft which still had caches of bombs on board. Even today you can see craters left by those bombs either side of major roads and rail networks. The scars of war never seem to fade on a landscape.

One day another local, Elizabeth Harrison (later to be Dick's wife), was involved in a riding accident and was seriously injured. She was immediately rushed to the Camp 250 hospital, where the German doctor got to work on her. Over a short space of time he tended to her wounds, cared for her and she was nursed back to health. Elizabeth was very grateful for the compassion shown from a man who belonged to what most people regarded as the enemy.

All in all, the Germans were remembered locally as being friendly and willing workers who helped out on the farms and businesses in the surrounding areas.

Karl Heinz Lessentin was a German prisoner of war based at the camp who was working at Springdale Farm. When in the years after the war's end all the German prisoners were heading back to Germany to be repatriated, Karl liked it so much that he chose to stay, and married local villager Nancy Ward. Rudston's one and only pub, the Bosville Arms, was used a lot by the British army and Karl was allowed to go there and enjoy his allowance of two pints of beer a day. All the prisoners who were allowed to go would soon be classed as regulars there, and it was there that he met Nancy.

Other villagers, such as local girl Grace Martin, used to get on well with the Germans and they even became quite popular. They got to the point where they were so comfortable being with the British that they even used to make things like toys and furniture from old bits of wood for their new friends. Much of it was expertly done, and you would never have guessed that it was made from old scrap wood.

At the beginning of September 1947, 100 extra men were loaned to Camp 250 from Camp 139, which was at Wolverton Hall, near Billingham, Durham. Their job was to help with the mammoth task of the harvest work in the district. This went on for only a few weeks maximum, and on 16th September the work was complete. As the tasks had been completed, the orders came through for 50 of the men to return the following day by train. After the hard work of the harvest they would most likely be looking forward to some well-earned rest back in Durham. They packed their bags up and got ready for the northbound trip, though not before they had had a good night's sleep.

* * * *

Wednesday 17th September 1947 was a normal day like any other, but with a bit more activity than usual at Camp 250 as everybody was up early to make sure the German prisoners got the early train from the nearest railway station at Burton Agnes back up the line to Durham.

One of those involved in getting the men to their destination was 21-year-old Roland Montague Cramer, who was a sergeant in the British Army, The Bedfordshire and Herts. regiment. The son of Alice and Montague C R Cramer of Monks Park, Wembley, Roland was looking forward to getting married in December. At the age of 14 he had been one of many thousands of children who had been evacuated at the outbreak of the war. With the rest of Kilburn Grammar School, they were all sent up to Northampton, where Roland very soon found that he wasn't really happy. His father, who had been in the army himself in the First World War, was a schoolmaster, and his school was evacuated at the same time, leaving both parents and Roland's nine-year-old brother Stanley starting their new temporary home living in a holiday camp at Bracklesham Bay near Chichester. Their mother Alice did not like the fact she had to stay there, so in the

April of 1940 all three of them went back down south to live in Wembley. Roland was to return back to his home around a month later to continue his studies at Wembley County School, where his brother Stanley describes him today as "a very sociable and sporty type" of lad who would gladly play football and cricket for the school teams.

As the Second World War was coming to an end, Roland was called up to join the army. Enthusiastic about his new job, his basic training led to a spiral of ideas he had which saw him begin training for the Parachute Regiment with a serious ambition to be involved in the gliders.

He enjoyed it immensely, but unfortunately for him, as the war ended in mid-1945 for both Germany and Japan, the army began cutting down on personnel. As a result his training was stopped and his army life began to turn another way. Before long he was receiving training to become a member of the "Beds and Herts" and sent up to Rudston to be based at the PoW camp.

He spent most of his time in the area around Bridlington, so he never really went home that much. His fiancée was living close by, so he was quite happy doing what he was doing. When he did make the occasional journey back to Wembley he never really spoke to anybody about what he did.

A lot of time had passed since he had joined the army and he was coming to the end of his National Service and expecting to be demobbed at some point soon. He didn't mind the army, but he did say that he would be glad to get back to being a civilian, even though he had nothing lined up as yet to look forward to.

Like anybody else in his situation, he was making the most of his life in the military and enjoying what he was doing. He had a lot to think about too: his wedding, a new job to find, where he was going to live with his new family. But all that was further down the line and he would worry about that nearer the time. A well-built man with a zest for life, he would have done well if he had joined the army during the conflict. Now he was in the same situation as thousands of others, going back to reality and returning to a normal civilian job.

Working closely that day with Roland was Staff Sgt James Wadey, a 26-year-old interpreter in the Royal Artillery, who was engaged to local girl Dorothy Warkup, who lived in the village of Lissett, just a few miles away. She was employed as a telephonist in Bridlington and they were also due to be married in the coming January of 1948. She had also just recently spent a holiday at James' home in London. James' job allocation in Rudston was to be the hostel NCO at Thorpe Hall on the camp.

Unfortunately Dorothy was no stranger to the

tragedy of conflict. At the height of the war she had been engaged to an RAF aircrew member stationed at Eden Camp, Malton. He was tragically killed during an air raid on the continent, leaving Dorothy devastated, but she regained her happiness later when she met and fell in love with James Wadey. They were looking forward to spending the rest of their lives together, and now the war was over it would all hopefully be plain sailing.

Parked up ready to be loaded was the vehicle they were to use to transport the prisoners. It was a 3-ton Bedford lorry (number L 1760191) with a canvas-covered body, fitted with a 27.9 horsepower engine and Lockheed hydraulic and vacuum servo brakes. The truck was inspected for its regular monthly routine overhaul at Royal Army Service Corps (RASC) workshops in York the day before and only two things had needed a bit of attention. First of all the exhaust required a touch of welding, then the handbrake needed adjusting slightly. It was nothing too serious and both repairs were carried out the same day before the lorry was successfully tested and returned to the camp.

Getting up extra early, the prisoners gathered their belongings up ready to leave, waiting for their turn to be driven away. At five o'clock that morning the truck was already loaded with personnel and their bags and departed the camp bound for the railway station at

Burton Agnes village, just a few miles away up the narrow country roads. At this time of the morning the whole area would seem deserted.

Hans Graf was a German prisoner who had a driving licence and was tasked to be the duty driver for the several trips it would take to get everybody safely to the station with their kit. Inside the cab was Staff Sgt Wadey, who was to assist with the search of kits before the prisoners left camp. He could drive a truck this size but he only held a military licence for motorcycles, Graf being the only authorised driver of the truck. Also in the cab was a second British soldier to be used as an official escort. Each trip would leave a small party of people with an escort on the station platform while the truck went back to pick up more.

Burton Agnes is a very small village just five miles south west of Bridlington. With one major road going directly through and a few country roads branching off, this was one place where nothing much ever seemed to happen. The station there consisted of two main signal boxes, one large, one small, with a platform on each side of the line but staggered to either side of the main road. Heading towards the crossing from the village you would be met by the station houses on your left with a platform over the crossing, whereas to your right would be the other platform on the nearside of the road. The railway line was used for both passenger trains and cargo, with livestock such as cattle and sheep being transported by train as well as much needed coal.

At 0530 the LNER (London and North Eastern Railway) signalman who was duty there, Miles William Gray, noticed the truck pull up at the station but not go over the crossing. It quickly unloaded its cargo of prisoners and kit, turned around and went away again within just a few minutes. The men would then collect their bags from the pile and make their way over to the platform to await their train. They had a while to wait yet, as there still needed to be further trips to get everybody down here. It was just a case of waiting for the time to come and hopefully the boredom would pass. Besides they would chat amongst each other as they normally would and most likely reminisce of their times in the war, their families back home and even going back to their normal camp.

In the meantime the truck was going back down the country lanes towards Rudston, where by 0550, with the first party already dropped off at the station, the truck had arrived back at the camp for a second load.

Meanwhile in Hull station, over 30 miles south of Burton Agnes, sat a train which was getting ready to depart. With steam already blowing out of its engines and the passengers safely sitting in their seats, the time was approaching for departure. Its destination was

Scarborough, around 50 miles north of where they were now. This was a regular journey taken every day by this train and countless others over the years. This one set of double lines connected the whole of the East Coast together, stopping at the major points at Beverley, Driffield and Bridlington as well as the smaller villages like Arram, Bempton, Hunmanby and Filey. Which villages you stopped at would depend on which timetable you were working on. Sometimes you would miss out most of them, while at other times the train would be scheduled to stop at them all. Either way, if you lived out in these sleepy dwellings there was a good chance that you would have the opportunity several times a day to travel to the major towns and cities.

At 0555, the LNER train slowly made its way out of the station and headed towards Scarborough. Driven by 52-year-old Charles Thomas Stephenson from Hull, the train was hauled by a D49/2 class 4-4-0 locomotive, number 2772, and consisted of a four-wheeled van behind the locomotive and five bogie coaches. The total weight of this workhorse was 255 tons. The locomotive was built in Darlington in January 1935, originally as No 374, and named the Sinnington after the North Yorkshire hunt. Designed by Sir Nigel Gresley, it had come from the last batch of the 3-cylinder Shire/Hunt class locomotives to be ordered. This type of train was popular and reliable, showing time and time again that there was never a job that they couldn't handle.

By now two lorryloads of PoWs had already been dropped off at Burton Agnes, including two Germans named Hoermann and Reichenbach. Together with their escort, a British soldier called Private Adams, they were now lining the platform waiting for the 0709 train that would take them to Selby, via Hull, where they would get their connecting train and head back up the line. This time when the truck went back for the next lorry load of POWs, it was driven by SSgt Wadey, closely watched by Hans Graf.

This wasn't the first time James Wadey had driven these vehicles; in fact there are people who say he had driven them several times before and was perfectly fine with them. Hopefully over the course of time he would be able to get his licence and be competent to drive them all the time.

Taking the country roads with ease, it didn't take long for Wadey to manoeuvre the truck round the narrow bends in the roads. After yet another short journey, the truck arrived back at the camp at 0620 and parked up to reload. As soon as they pulled up there was a small army of prisoners already waiting with their belongings eager to jump aboard.

Meanwhile over at the railway station, the crowd of

Germans on the platform were counting the minutes until they were able to get seated on the train and start their journey properly. Masses of kitbags were piled up around the prisoners; some of them would have been sent over without their owners so that they could fit more in the back of the truck later. It wouldn't be long now before they were all reunited with their bags and together again.

Time was ticking on and it was a case of constantly checking the hour. As it was getting towards the winter months, it would have been cold that time of the morning, the sun not having had chance to heat up the land and spread the warm rays around. Standing and looking over the fields, the soldiers would have seen a beautiful sight this early - sunrise over the cold landscape, the complete silence in the absence of traffic broken only by the singing birds. No matter which way you looked at it, there were definitely worse places to spend your life as a prisoner.

In the meantime, over the road in the station house, people were starting to arrive at work. Campbell John was one of them. He was a 42-year-old railway porter who worked at the Burton Agnes station house, and at 0615 he arrived early, as usual, to start his shift. There were several other people there today, as was normal for the routines that were run on village stations.

In charge of it all was stationmaster Mr Frederick

James Dixon who lived there with his family. There was only one signalman in the box, Miles William Gray, the second member of that team being George Howden, but he would not be seen today as he was having his day off. A small village railway station had to run like clockwork, because if it didn't the emphasis of the jobs in hand would be placed on others who already had more than one important task to do.

Thankfully the people who worked here were a friendly bunch and professional. During the height of the war a story was told of how a train had stopped at this very station and somebody ran out of the main building shouting for everybody to get off. The train was evacuated and everybody ran into the fields, and seconds later a German aircraft swooped low and riddled the carriages with gunfire. Nobody was even injured, thanks to the quick wit of a very observant member of the team.

A few miles back down the road, back at the Rudston camp, the truck was once again fully loaded and ready to go. Wadey got in the drivers seat, the German driver Hans Graf occupied the middle seat and Sgt Cramer got into the front left hand side. Cramer was the escort in charge of the new batch of prisoners now being driven. With 25 in the back and Graf, Wadey and Cramer in the front, the truck departed for the final trip. Not one prisoner had left the camp on foot, the normal practice being to walk there instead of being driven.

* * * *

At the approach to the station at Burton Agnes, just 202 yards away from the line, there is a sign saying "Gated Level Crossing Ahead". These gates had been closed by Signalman Gray at 0635 for an up line train, which had come and gone. The gates remained closed, as just seven minutes later there would be a down train from Hull to Bridlington; on this occasion it would be the one driven by Charles Stephenson. Although it was not due to stop there, it would be going past at full speed, around 60 mph.

Gray waited for the minutes to pass and sure enough the locomotive was seen approaching as expected. Thundering down the tracks trailing smoke and steam, the Sinnington was on time and loaded with passengers who had been picked up from several stations since the train had left Hull.

Lorry driver Stanley Mackenzie had left his home in Haisthorpe, just a few miles up the road, at about 0620 on a motorcycle, bound for his workplace in Catfoss. As he approached Burton Agnes crossing heading towards the village, he noticed the gates were closed, so he stopped his motorcycle and side car with the front wheel near the centre of the gates and began to wait patiently for the Scarborough-bound train to pass before carrying on his journey.

At 0642 the train could be heard speeding down the line, but at the same time coming down the main road towards the station was the army truck driven by Wadey, going at around 30 mph. As the vehicle approached the crossing the engine was suddenly heard to start "racing", as if the truck had been given a sudden acceleration. Without slowing down, the vehicle was seen to be heading straight for the railway line.

Instead of stopping gently at the opposite gates, Mackenzie was horrified to see the front of the truck smash through the gate and come to a sudden standstill right on the railway line. Now the scene was set for an unimaginable disaster.

Chapter 3

Impact

As the truck came to a halt amid broken pieces of wood from the crossing gate, the occupants had no time to react. With the train just a few yards away and bearing down on them at full speed, a collision was unavoidable.

On board the train, standing behind the driver, 24-year-old fireman Kenneth Robinson saw the lorry crash through onto the line and brought his head back into the cabin so he would not see the impact. The men in the back would have felt the jolt of the initial crash through the gates and were probably wondering what they had hit.

What they didn't know for those few split seconds was that worse was to come.

The station porter, Campbell John, explained later: "The gates had been closed several minutes when I saw the train rapidly approaching and the lorry, filled with German prisoners, drive up to the crossing. I realised the driver of the lorry could not stop in time." With no time to reverse or even carry on forward, the truck sat there like a child's toy. The front of the train slammed into the truck's bonnet at around 55 mph, forcing the whole vehicle against the side of the crossing gate, which was carried with them together along the line, tearing up the fencing at the side of the station, while the brickwork of the smaller signal cabin was hit and badly damaged. (According to the porter the signal box windows were smashed too.)

John would not be allowed to leave his post to render assistance, as the line was still open and work had to be done to stop other trains hitting the wreckage. Not only had a disaster occurred, but it was now his job to make sure another one didn't follow it.

The truck had been ripped into nothing more than scrap metal and matchwood, the largest piece of wreckage being the rear axle and wheels, which came to rest at the end of the houses 60 yards down the line from the crossing. Various pieces of debris were strewn up the line for a further 200 yards, personal items littering the track - boots, clothing and army kit. One was a personal letter addressed to a Gerd Betfry at the Rudston camp.

Incredibly, nobody on the train was injured, nor was it derailed, although the collision caused it to rock badly, coming to a stop just down the line with only minor damage.

As shock set in among those who had just witnessed the collision, it became apparent that there were survivors who needed medical treatment as quickly as possible.

The rescue operation now had to begin. With the dead and injured littering the tracks it was in some cases hard to find out if people were dead or just unconscious. Most of those who were still alive were moaning in agony as they lay surrounded by the scattered limbs of their dead comrades. Those who were already on the platform with their British escort raced down onto the tracks to give assistance. Working together as a team, they began by carrying the injured into the station waiting room and giving first aid where it was needed. Sheets were torn up to make dressings, while blankets were taken from the house to be used on those who would now be suffering from shock and whose body temperature would now be plummeting. Others made the survivors tea from their rations, another effect of the war that would be felt until the mid-1950s. It was important to keep the people warm, and with the cold of the morning it was crucial that they were kept awake and wrapped up; the last thing they wanted was to save a life and survive only to die from intense cold. The body would immediately start shivering, and even if it had been a baking hot day the result would have been the same.

Although the alarm was raised straight away, it would be around 30 minutes before ambulances reached the scene. Two doctors from Bridlington, Dr Watson and Dr Webster, rushed straight there. Racing into the waiting room, they immediately got to work and started tending to the wounded.

On the track itself, single-line work was put into operation immediately to keep the trains running, but only once the dead and injured had been recovered and the slight damage to the sleepers and fixings had been repaired.

At 7 am the Malton to Bridlington train came to a slow stop at the station and transferred the passengers from the collision train to get them all out of the way and onwards to their destination.

23-year-old clerk Josie Jennings, who had been working at the station since 1942, was due to come on for her duty at 8 am. She lived at the nearby Post Office with her family, her mother being the postmistress while her father was the village joiner. When she arrived at the crossing she was greeted with a scene of absolute chaos. She wondered what had happened. The crash had been so quick that very few people even knew anything had happened, the road to the crossing being pretty well deserted of houses.

Josie saw that there were ambulances all around and pieces of random wreckage strewn on the line, while people were running about to get the injured in a good position to be able to be moved to the hospitals. Something had happened here, and it was something big.

Straight away she was ushered into the station master's house instead of her usual office so that she would not see the carnage outside. She then stayed there with Mr Dixon's wife, their daughter (Mrs A Page) and daughter in-law (Mrs V Dixon) while the clean-up operation commenced. Mrs Page had looked out of her window in horror and seen the wreckage, noticing what looked like the driver still in what was left of the cab, dead. The whole family had all been woken by the crash, as they had still been asleep in bed. She recalls over 60 years later that it took a long time to clear up the wreckage and was amazed by the fact that 16 people had in fact survived the crash.

By the time Mrs Page actually got to do her work that day, all the survivors had been taken away. Eight had been taken to Bridlington's Lloyd Hospital, four of them being transferred to Beverley; one of these was a survivor named only as Minkus, aged 23, who had both his legs amputated. Two more were taken to Driffield Base hospital. All the injured had been taken away from the scene by 8 am, just in time for Josie to see the last of them leave. The death toll was two British soldiers - James Wadey and Roland Cramer - and seven German prisoners killed instantly, while three more Germans died soon afterwards in hospital.

For 12 people to be killed on such a quiet country crossing was shocking. Of all the places for it to happen - why here? After surviving the years of war - the bombings, the shootings, the explosions - why did they all have to die in a tragic accident at this sleepy little village?

20-year-old Keith Hawkins, the cousin of Josie Jennings, also lived at the Post Office and was cycling to Stud Farm, where he was working as an apprentice. The journey took him over the level crossing, and although he did not hear the initial crash he approached the site later on that morning to find a scene of army and police personnel all over, the crossing gate well and truly smashed up, and pieces of wreckage all around the tracks heading down the line towards Bridlington. He didn't stop to have a proper look as he was waved on by those at the scene, and he went to work as normal.

A local council truck driver named Tom Dolphin was stopped by the police a few miles away and asked if he could head over to Burton Agnes railway station as there had been a crash. They needed anybody they could get hold of to assist with the clear up, and his truck would definitely be key to helping with that. He would tell his son years later that those Germans who were alive (most likely those already on the platform at the time) had to throw severed limbs into the back of the truck and have them rushed to Bridlington. The back axle meanwhile, which had come to rest at the side of the line around 60 yards from the crossing, was later hauled away by a farm tractor.

The crash only smashed one gate of the four at the level crossing, and incredibly this was replaced just 24 hours later. The actual railway line was pretty much undamaged and after slight repairs the line was re-opened soon after for trains to continue as normal.

Chapter 4

Picking up the pieces

By that evening the word had got out about the disaster. The Hull Daily Mail had the first headlines - "Hull Train Hits Lorry at Crossing – Twelve Die" - and reporters got a first-hand account from one eyewitness on the scene: "I was standing on the platform near the signal box when the lorry crashed through the closed gates and on to the line. The express was only a short distance away travelling at full speed. There was a terrific noise and screams from the engine whistle as the train hit the lorry. The train carried the lorry along and the main post of the railway gates was uprooted and a hole made in the side of the signal box."

A woman called Catherine Wilson who lived nearly three miles away heard about the disaster, and she would enter in her diary: "There has been an awful accident at Burton Agnes station. A lorry load of prisoners went through the gate and an express train ran into it. I think 13 (sic) have died up to now."

SSgt Wadey's fiancée, Dorothy Warkup, was at work in Bridlington when she heard the news. She was led away in a distressed state and allowed to go home immediately, as this was her second fiancé to die tragically in just a few years.

It was not so subtle for the family of Roland Cramer in Wembley. Roland's 16-year-old brother Stan was alone in the house by himself while his parents had gone to the cinema together, which was something they rarely did. That evening it wasn't an official that broke the news to Stan, but a reporter from a London evening newspaper, who came to the door and told him of the crash and of his brother's death. It was already headlines in the papers and that was the first he had heard about it; there had been nothing official from anybody.

When his parents came back he had to be the one to break the bad news to them. Needless to say they were in a state of overwhelming shock, and it took a long time for the news to actually sink in. How could this be? He was only up in Yorkshire! There were far more dangerous things he had wanted to do in the army, but once again a tragic accident had robbed another family of their son and sibling.

Now the clean-up operation was complete,

investigators had to find out why this had happened. The inquest, conducted by Mr H. W. Rennison, the deputy coroner for the East Riding, was opened on 18 September 1947 for identification purposes only and adjourned until 4 pm on Thursday 2 October. The prisoners of war were identified by Gunther Hoermann, who was assisted by a German interpreter, while the two British soldiers were identified by RSM C. Smallwood of Camp 250, Rudston. A representative of LNER, Mr A E Boothroyd, expressed sympathy on behalf of the company, and said that although the blame did not lie with LNER, they were still obliged to offer any assistance with the inquiry they could.

When the inquest was resumed, Captain H. C. Holmes, who was the commanding officer of Camp 250, revealed that the prisoners should have actually walked from the camp to the train station. Transport was provided for the baggage, but the prisoners should have walked the three and a half miles on foot. If they had stuck to protocol, then they would all have lived; Graf would have been driving and Cramer would have been escorting on foot. But with every tragedy, it is easy to be wise after the event.

* * * *

The funeral of the ten Germans was held in

Bridlington on 22 September 1947 and attended by around 2000 people, among them hundreds of prisoners from camps around the area. The service was conducted in German by Dr J Rieger as well as by German padres F. Gebhardt (Protestant) and Spuelbeck (Catholic). Also in attendance were British army officers in charge of Camp 250, including the Commandant, Lt Col J L G Marjoribanks Egerton, the Commandant of Camp 139, Major Covenay, the Mayor and Mayoress of Bridlington, Councillor and Mrs F F Millner, the Rev N A Vasey, the Vicar Of Christ Church, and Inspector H H Walker, representing Bridlington police. A choir from 136 Camp at Welton Hall, near Brough, took part in the service.

In his address, Rev Vasey expressed sympathy to those affected and said that on behalf of Bridlington Council of Churches he had sent letters to all the relatives of those who had died at Burton Agnes. He gave thanks for the hard work that these men had done in the fields and extended the hand of friendship to all those involved in such tasks.

Each coffin was brought from the mortuary in Bridlington town to the cemetery at Sewerby Road, where it was borne by four prisoners of war, each with a 5th following behind carrying a wreath. They slowly passed through two lines of other prisoners as they entered the cemetery grounds. There was a long line of wreaths and flowers from locals and other dignitaries who wanted to pay their respects. The coffins were then lowered into the ground, after a small orchestra of prisoners of war had played Handel's Largo by the graveside. The rows of graves were decorated with floral tributes, so much so that it was hard to see any space in between. These men had worked together, travelled together and died together.

An appeal by the Bridlington Council of Churches Prisoner of War Social Centre Committee ended up with 53 people donating gifts of rationed food and clothing for the relatives of those killed, with 21 separate seven-pound food parcels making their way to the bereaved relatives.

* * * *

The official inquiry into what happened that day at Burton Agnes was conducted by Lt Col E Woodhouse of the Ministry of Transport at York. He had viewed the scene soon after the crash and begun gathering evidence, speaking to eyewitnesses, locals and experts. Police Constable R Waddingham of Burton Agnes said at the time that the accident had happened in daylight with good visibility, and the road surface was good and dry. The truck driver would have seen the crossing from 175 yards away, but there was no suggestion that the brakes had been applied. In fact two injured survivors, named Schlupper and Jungblut, said at the inquiry that the journey was "unusually fast", causing prisoners to be thrown about on bends. There was no sensation of the truck braking just before impact. They all agreed that the vehicle did not slow down but did feel the engine "racing" in the final moment. This fits in with the story told by Stan Mackenzie, who had stopped his bike at the crossing.

As for the train itself, the inquiry pointed out that buffer locking took place at the rear of the four wheel van and one pair of its wheels actually left the track a short distance down the line before re-railing themselves about 90 yards down at a diamond crossing. The brakes on the train were tested after the accident and found to be in good working order still. It was this part of the story that makes one realise how bad it could have been should the train have derailed and come completely off the tracks. Full of passengers and going at full speed, this could very easily have turned to an even bigger tragedy with a larger death toll and an untold number of injuries. Thankfully the weight of the train and its design ensured that it escaped from such a predicament.

Woodhouse concluded: "The arrangement and spacing of the control pedals of the Bedford three-tonner is such that if a driver is unfamiliar with the vehicle it is easy for his right foot to slip from the brake pedal to the accelerator close alongside, or for him to apply the brake and depress the accelerator at the same time. This might well account for the racing of the engine at the last moment... though the driver's seat is movable, it takes a little time to adjust it. It transpired that Wadey was some inches taller than Graf and he thought that an uncomfortable and inconvenient driving position would make slipping of the driver's foot from the brake pedal to the accelerator more likely."

Chapter 5

Burial and remembrance

After an investigation lasting just two months, Lt Col Woodhouse came to the conclusion that the cause was the "careless handling of the lorry by an unauthorised and apparently inexperienced driver, Staff-Sgt Wadey." The report was submitted to the Ministry of Transport on 29 October 1947.

The accident was described by the Chief Constable of the East Riding as "probably the most serious accident involving a road vehicle which has ever occurred in this country." It put the accident statistics of the area at an all-time high, with 13 deaths recorded in the September, 12 of them from the crash at Burton Agnes.

With the inquest and the inquiry having reached a satisfactory conclusion, the investigation was now over.

* * * *

The German war cemetery at Cannock Chase in Staffordshire was established under the terms of an agreement concluded on 16th October 1959 between the British Government and the Federal Republic of Germany. On behalf of Germany, the Volksbund Deutsche Kriegsgraber-fürsorge (German War Graves Commission) undertook the task of designing and constructing a cemetery to which the bodies of most of the German war dead would be subsequently transferred from various sites around the UK, so that they would be placed in one area. This would give the families of those Germans who had died overseas a single place to go to remember their loved ones. At least in the United Kingdom most of them would be in the one cemetery.

Most of the dead Germans in the UK had died in prisoner-of-war camps, but there were a few who were washed ashore or died in air crashes during the war itself. Of the 4940 war victims buried at Cannock Chase, 2143 died in WW1, 2797 in WW2. All around the country graves were exhumed and the remains taken to Cannock Chase, where memorial stones were erected on each grave bearing the name and dates. Amongst the Germans to be listed as being reburied were the ten prisoners of war from Bridlington Cemetery.

On 22 June 1962 the teams of gravediggers came to Bridlington Cemetery and headed towards the central area where the ten Germans who had died at Burton Agnes were at rest. They were exhumed one by one from their plots in the cemetery and loaded up to be taken down the country to be reburied at the new cemetery in Cannock Chase, where they remain to this day.

22-year-old Vera West was a local girl who had heard about the disaster and felt so sorry for those injured that she took the time to visit them in hospital to give them a bit of moral support and cheer them up. One of these was the man who had lost both his legs. Friendships blossomed and she became very good acquaintances with them all, even keeping in touch with two of the survivors all her life (one of whom wanted to marry her) and getting regular Christmas cards and letters from them. She died in January 2012.

Staff Sgt James Wadey was taken to his home city and buried in Tower Hamlets Cemetery in east London on 25 September 1947. The site is today is a nature reserve overgrown with plant life and bushes, a home to much wildlife and cared for by a trust. It is this 33-acre broadleaf woodland that will prevents the graves being flattened and covered over forever. Many of the graves have historical significance, so much so that the Friends of Tower Hamlets Cemetery Park run tours for those interested parties who want to see what has been described as "an outstanding variety of wild plants and animals".

Amongst the graves there are victims of the sinking of the Thames river boat Princess Alice, which was split in two in a collision in September 1878, with the deaths of around 640 passengers. That shipwreck has gone down in history as one of the most notorious inland disasters in the UK, with it being so close to the river side.

Like Wadey, Sgt Roland Cramer was also taken back south and buried in London, at the Alperton Cemetery in the west of the city, near his home. Although he was a popular man, there were few people at the ceremony as he was not widely known in the area, all his school friends having been scattered around the country over the years and his comrades still working up north in Yorkshire. It was a small funeral, with just neighbours and close family turning up to pay their respects. His aunt provided comfort to his mother; she was still in a state of much distress and could not believe that her son would never be coming home again. Now and again the family would talk about the regret they felt at not seeing him as much over the years. Like many a war story, it was too late to do anything about it. Today Roland Cramer has a standard commonwealth gravestone, with his name, service number and regiment engraved in a whitewashed stone. The site and area are tended regularly.

Josie Jennings went back to work as normal,

shocked by what had happened in her little station. Over the years she saw several German survivors return to thank the railways and station staff for their life-saving actions that day. She would continue to work at the station until 1951, when she would move down south.

The locomotive which collided with the truck, number 2772, later became No 62772 and carried on its normal journeys in the Yorkshire area until it was finally withdrawn from the Selby shed in the September of 1958.

Burton Agnes railway station closed for good on 5th January 1970 after being active for 124 years. The station buildings were sold off and are today private houses. Over the years the main signal tower has been demolished and the smaller signal box, which was built in 1870, is now a listed building, restored by its current owner, Roger Moreton. The old station is now a group of three large houses which now and then get strange happenings in the middle of the night. Residents over the years report random bangs being heard on the door and on several occasions the occupier has come downstairs to see a man standing in the back yard wearing an old-style army uniform that has long been replaced. The man then vanishes into thin air as if he had never been there. Most people would discount this as the result of tiredness or your eyes playing tricks on you, but several people unconnected to each other have seen this with no explanation and no knowledge of the disaster that occurred there in 1947.

Camp 250 was slowly taken apart over the years when the use of a prisoner-of-war shelter was no longer needed. Only a few small parts of the camp are still visible today; for example as you head out of Rudston away from the coastal end there is a concrete section of layby at the side of the road which today is pretty much all that remains of this forgotten piece of local history. It is an area that farmers use for parking their trucks and dumping piles of manure. Very little remains, and there is nothing to commemorate what went on here except the memories of the few locals who were there at the time.

One German prisoner of war to return was Karl Lessantin, who came back to Bridlington in 1985 to see the graves of his dead comrades. He went straight to the site, but there was just grass. It took a while to find out, via his son John contacting the Beverley archive offices, that the bodies had been exhumed in the 1960s and taken to the war graves cemetery in Cannock Chase. Until recently the photos John took in 1947 of the ten graves covered in wreaths and flowers had remained lost, until he found them again in his family attic in Germany during a visit in Christmas 2013.

Those photos were sent to me just in time for this book to be published.

* * * *

So now it comes to my personal connection to the Burton Agnes crash. To be honest I had never heard of it, and neither had 99% of people who lived nearby. A few railway enthusiasts and local historians had read the report, and that is about it. But it was my research into the Lockington rail crash of 1986 that brought this disaster to my attention. For just over a year, back in 2009/2010, I successfully campaigned for a memorial to the nine people who died when a train was derailed at a level crossing just 15 miles up the line from Burton Agnes, heading towards Hull. An old shut-down railway station just like this one, Lockington had the same kind of country crossing, but due to British Rail cuts, the barriers had been taken away. A small van accidentally strayed onto the line and was hit by a modern four-car train full of people heading to Hull for the day.

The stories I found about this disaster were both incredible and heroic. But it was my connections to a few people that first brought Burton Agnes to my attention. When I read the report for the first time I was amazed that something so big could go unnoticed in the history books. I spoke to Lockington survivor Richard Myerscough, who told me that there had been a prisoner-of-war camp at Rudston and a further chat with a friend of mine who had been a train driver on that very line told me about the scale of the disaster.

It seemed wrong that so many people could die and nothing be done to remember this. All 12 victims were now buried far away, the station was closed and apart from a few articles in the newspapers from years back there was nothing to even suggest it had happened. Nobody really knew about the wartime stories in the area, and certainly not about a collision.

Richard Myerscough and I started doing research into what happened. While he looked into the camp and the German graves, I concentrated on the background to the crash itself. I found that a brass memorial plaque was put in the chapel at Eden Camp in Malton, now a history museum dedicated to the war, but there was nothing to suggest anything had happened at the crossing and very little information was available. The crossing was quieter now than it had been back in the war, with the usual few trains that go past every hour and the odd farm machinery and car passing through. However, I began putting the feelers out to see what the general opinion was of having a plaque up somewhere close by to commemorate what happened.

My first thought was to try and get a plaque of some sort up at the war memorial on the main road. That way wreaths could be laid and lives remembered on Remembrance Sunday every year. When I contacted the parish council, the woman I spoke to said quite definitely and finally that they didn't want a memorial to Germans next to the village war memorial. I wanted this opinion in writing, but when I wrote to them on two occasions the parish council did not reply (despite them telling the local newspapers that they had). I then contacted Burton Agnes Hall, a stately home with a lot of history and huge gardens, being quite a tourist attraction in the summer with the Hall, gardens, tea room, gift shop and even an English Heritage medieval manor house in the grounds. They too were not willing to help, their reply being "we do understand the importance of remembering and marking historical events, however we would be unable to have a memorial in the grounds of the Hall. We receive many requests and unfortunately we have to be fair and say no to them all."

But it wasn't all unsuccessful. Thankfully the local press were on my side and were interested in what I was talking about. The two main ones, the Bridlington Free Press and the Hull Daily Mail, both ran good articles on my campaign, which was excellent for the publicity and even led to a few people coming forward with information. One of those who got in touch was a woman named Linda Millard from Wigan. She said that she believed that the German victim Hans Graf, who was killed in the truck's cab, was her father, her birth occurring slightly over nine months after her mother had last seen him before he died. She was more than happy to contribute funds towards the memorial plaque and took a keen interest in developments.

In between running several other projects, including putting up a memorial to another major rail disaster, the Moorgate tube crash of 1975, I managed to speak with the owners of the houses which used to be the old railway station at the Burton Agnes crossing. They were all very interested in what was being said, and that is where I met Roger Moreton. He had recently bought the old signal box, which was now classed as a listed building. He had restored it himself back to its original specifications and condition and contacted the relevant authorities to gain permission for a plaque to go up on the side of the building. I had sent the design of the plaque to him and they seemed more than happy with that. Permission was granted without any problems, and the only task then was to actually have the plaque made.

While I was doing all this I decided to set up a group on the social networking site Facebook to honour those who lived and died that day and hopefully find people who had stories to tell about the crash or if anybody was interested in learning about this forgotten piece of history. I was more than happy that within days several interested people had joined it and wanted to be kept up to date with developments.

Roger, meanwhile, was hunting around for a good stonemason to do the plaque and surprised me within weeks by having it made and put up for quite a good price! The making of the plaque went ahead and I was happy that I could then organise a short ceremony to have an official unveiling.

I started by inviting the people who had helped with the few stories that were available, contacting Linda Millard, John Lessentin and a few other locals who were interested. I decided to arrange it for Monday 23rd December 2013. It was unfortunately too late to have it on the September 17th anniversary, but I was still able to get it sorted before the end of the year. I contacted the local Royal British Legion, who had Martin Barmby ring me back to organise the ceremony. After a long chat with him it turned out that he was an ex-Royal Navy sailor, and suddenly we found we had more in common that just an interest in local military history! After discussing what was required to honour the 12 killed at Burton Agnes, the day was planned.

* * * *

It was 2 pm, on a very wet and windy afternoon, Monday 23rd December 2013, with around 20 people gathered at the old signal box for the short unveiling service. Despite the conditions, there were standard bearers from the Royal British Legion either side of the signal box door, one member standing alone ready to unveil the plaque.

Getting everybody's attention, I stood up to briefly tell the story of why we were here today and to show people the exact point of impact that shattered so many lives in just a few seconds. A speech by Lockington survivor Richard Myerscough told the story of how he had heard about the crash himself and why he wanted to be here today. He mentioned the previous work we had done together to get their memorial up in 2010 and ended by telling the story of how his friend in Germany had done some research which led me to visit the graves at Cannock Chase.

Then came the moment where the cameras all pointed at the signal box. Alex Morris of the Royal British Legion slowly peeled back the protective covering, unveiling the brand new plaque. The next few minutes were nothing more than the noise of cameras clicking as locals and a press photographer wanted to capture the moment themselves. Then came the realisation that these names were real people, who had had real lives, careers, families and stories.

I stood back in front of the small crowd and once again got their attention. It was then, for the first time in 66 years, that the names of all 12 victims were read out, by myself. We then held a minute's silence and took that time to reflect on the tragedy, and how it had been, up until now, another forgotten incident lost to history. We thought of the people who went to war and never returned; those who had never been recovered. Through their sacrifices we live in a free country today.

A few minutes later the ceremony was over. A few questions by locals and the press, and we were all on our way. Thankfully the rain held off for those few minutes and the plaque was once again left alone and in peace, next to the railway crossing which is now no longer a forgotten disaster.

As the old eulogy goes which is recited every Remembrance Day - in the morning and at the going down of the sun, we will remember them.

This story would not have been possible without the kind help
of a number of people and organisations.

Roger Moreton
Tom Dolphin
Keith Hawkins
Joan Tindall
Stanley Cramer
Cath Wilson
John Lessantin
Richard Myerscough
Ken Tunstall
Mike Wilson
Herman Engelmayer
Rosie Mitchinson and the Rudston news letter
Carol and Bill Lincoln
John Musk
Alex Schofield

Eden Camp modern history theme museum
Bridlington Library
Hull Daily Mail
Malton Gazette and Herald
Bridlington Free Press
National Railway museum/Science and Society picture library
Friends of Tower Hamlets Cemetery
Royal British Legion (Bridlington branch)
Royal Artillery

The official accident report is still available online free at the
Railways Archive, an excellent website for any railway enthusiast or
if you want information on historic railway mishaps.

ND - #0449 - 270225 - C12 - 203/127/5 - PB - 9781861511966 - Matt Lamination